Easy to Intermediate Piano Solo

THE WORLD'S GREAT CLASSICA

Great Easier Piano Literature

95 Favorite Selections of Original Music for Piano

Easy to Intermediate Piano Solo

EDITED BY BLAKE NEELY AND RICHARD WALTERS

Cover Paintings: Sanraedam, *St. Margs* Church, 1662

ISBN 978-0-7935-8257-0

Copyright © 1998 by HAL LEONARD LLC
International Copyright Secured All Rights Reserved

Visit Hal Leonard Online at
www.halleonard.com

Contact us:
Hal Leonard
7777 West Bluemound Road
Milwaukee, WI 53213
Email: info@halleonard.com

In Europe, contact:
Hal Leonard Europe Limited
42 Wigmore Street
Marylebone, London, W1U 2RN
Email: info@halleonardeurope.com

In Australia, contact:
Hal Leonard Australia Pty. Ltd.
4 Lentara Court
Cheltenham, Victoria, 3192 Australia
Email: info@halleonard.com.au

CONTENTS

Solfeggietto

Carl Philipp Emanuel Bach
1714-1788

Non troppo vivo

Little Prelude No. 2 in C Major

Johann Sebastian Bach
1685-1750

Moderato

Little Prelude No. 3 in C Minor

Johann Sebastian Bach
1685-1750

[Allegro con moto]

[*mp*]

[cresc.]

[f]

[decresc.]

10

Little Prelude No. 7 in E Minor

Johann Sebastian Bach
1685-1750

Little Prelude No. 8 in F Major

Johann Sebastian Bach
1685-1750

[Allegro]

[mf]

[_____ f]

Musette in G Major
from English Suite No. 3

Johann Sebastian Bach
1685-1750

March in D Major
from the LITTLE CLAVIER BOOK FOR ANNA MAGDALENA BACH

Johann Sebastian Bach
1685-1750

Marcato

Minuet in G Major
from the LITTLE CLAVIER BOOK FOR ANNA MAGDALENA BACH

Johann Sebastian Bach
1685-1750

Allegretto

Musette in D Major
from the LITTLE CLAVIER BOOK FOR ANNA MAGDALENA BACH

Johann Sebastian Bach
1685-1750

Round Dance
No. 8 from GYERMEKEKNEK (For Children)

Béla Bartók
1881-1945
Sz. 42

Allegretto

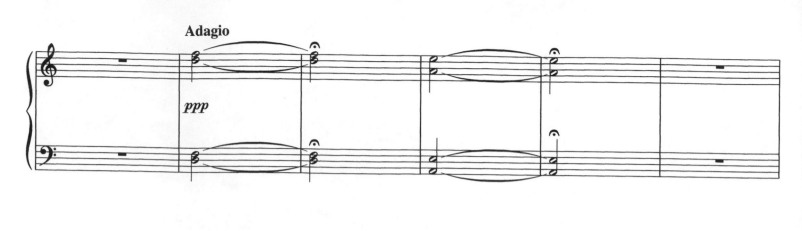

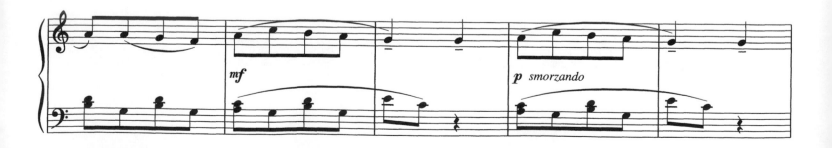

Alone in the Rain

No. 10 from GYERMEKEKNEK (For Children)

Béla Bartók
1881-1945
Sz. 42

Allegro molto

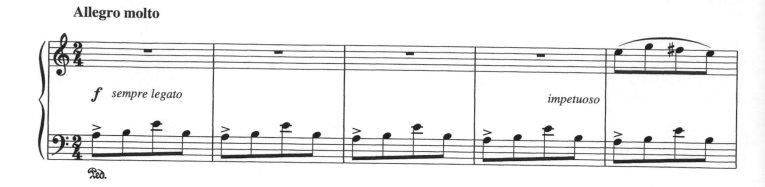

Circle Dance

No. 5 from GYERMEKEKNEK (For Children)

Béla Bartók
1881-1945
Sz. 42

Poco Allegretto

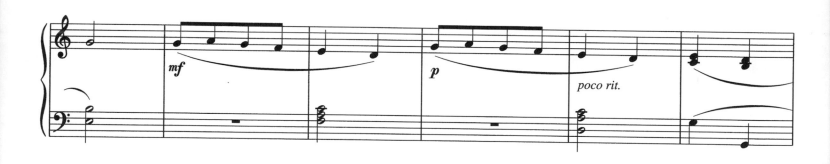

Poco più vivo

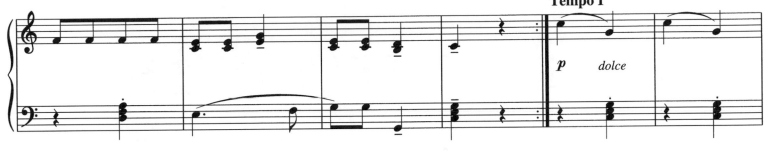

The Flowers Sing of Love
No. 6 from GYERMEKEKNEK (For Children)

Béla Bartók
1881-1945
Sz. 42

Allegro

Forward March
No. 27 from GYERMEKEKNEK (For Children)

Béla Bartók
1881-1945
Sz. 42

Allegramente

Ecossaise in E-flat Major

Ludwig van Beethoven
1770-1827
WoO 86

29

Ecossaise in G Major

Ludwig van Beethoven
1770-1827
WoO 23

Allegretto

Minuet in G Major

Ludwig van Beethoven
1770-1827

TRIO

Für Elise
(For Elise)

Ludwig van Beethoven
1770-1827
WoO 59

Sonata in G Major

Ludwig van Beethoven
1770-1827
Op. 49, No. 2

Allegro ma non troppo (♩ = 84-88)

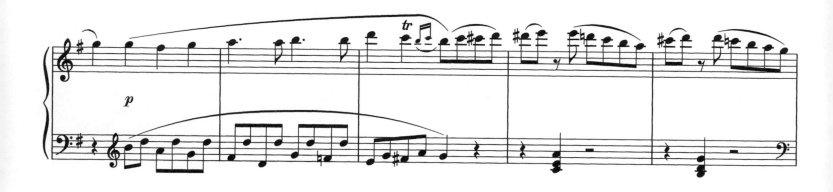

Tempo di Minuetto (♩ = 112-116)

Sonata in G Minor

Ludwig van Beethoven
1770-1827
Op. 49, No. 1

54

56

RONDO

Allegro (♩. = 112)

60

Arabesque

Friedrich Burgmüller
1806-1874
Op. 100, No. 2

Inquiétude

Friedrich Burgmüller
1806-1874
Op. 100, No. 18

Pastorale

Friedrich Burgmüller
1806-1874
Op. 100, No. 3

Prelude in A Major

Fryderyk Chopin
1810-1849
Op. 28, No. 7

Prelude in B Minor

Fryderyk Chopin
1810-1849
Op. 28, No. 6

Lento assai

Prelude in E Minor

Fryderyk Chopin
1810-1849
Op. 28, No. 4

Largo

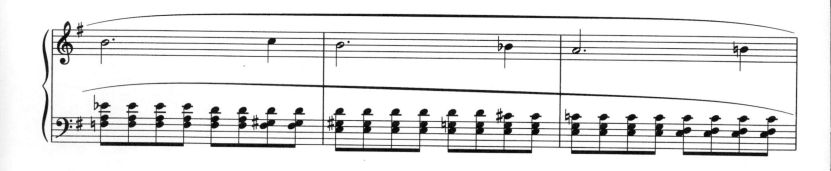

Prelude in C Minor

Fryderyk Chopin
1810–1849
Op. 28, No. 20

Sonatina in C Major

Muzio Clementi
1752-1832
Op. 36, No. 1

Spiritoso

Andante

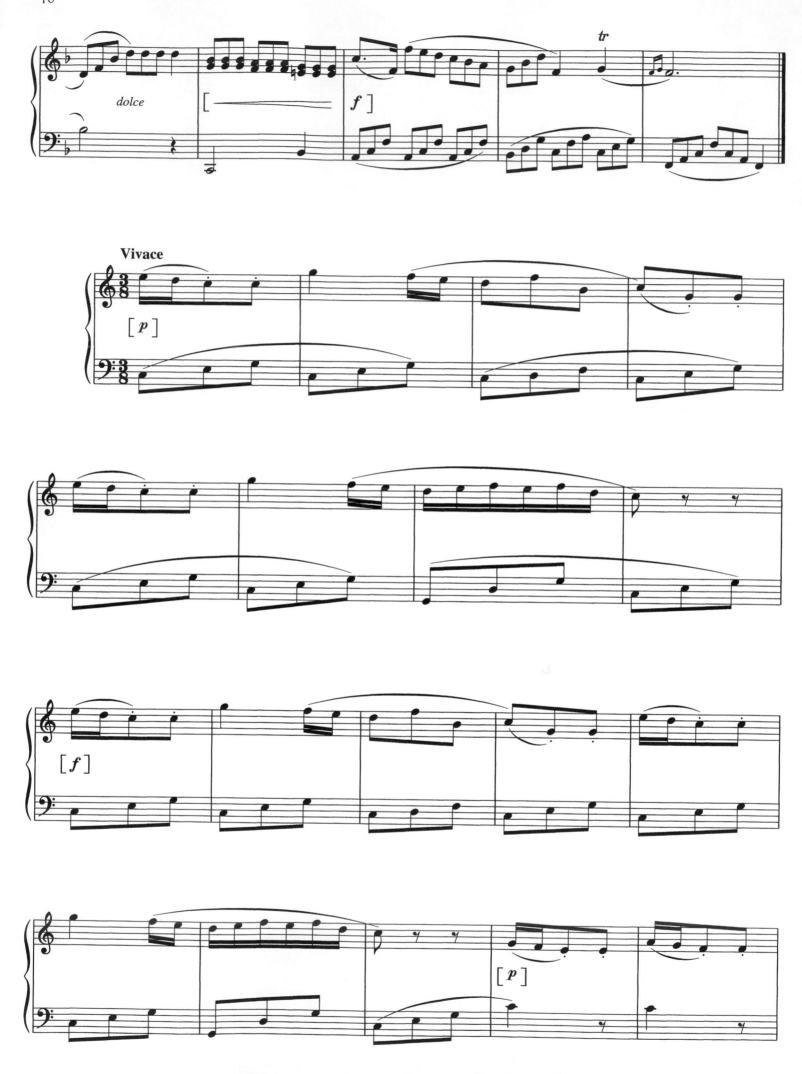

Sonatina in C Major

Muzio Clementi
1752-1832
Op. 36, No. 3

Un poco adagio

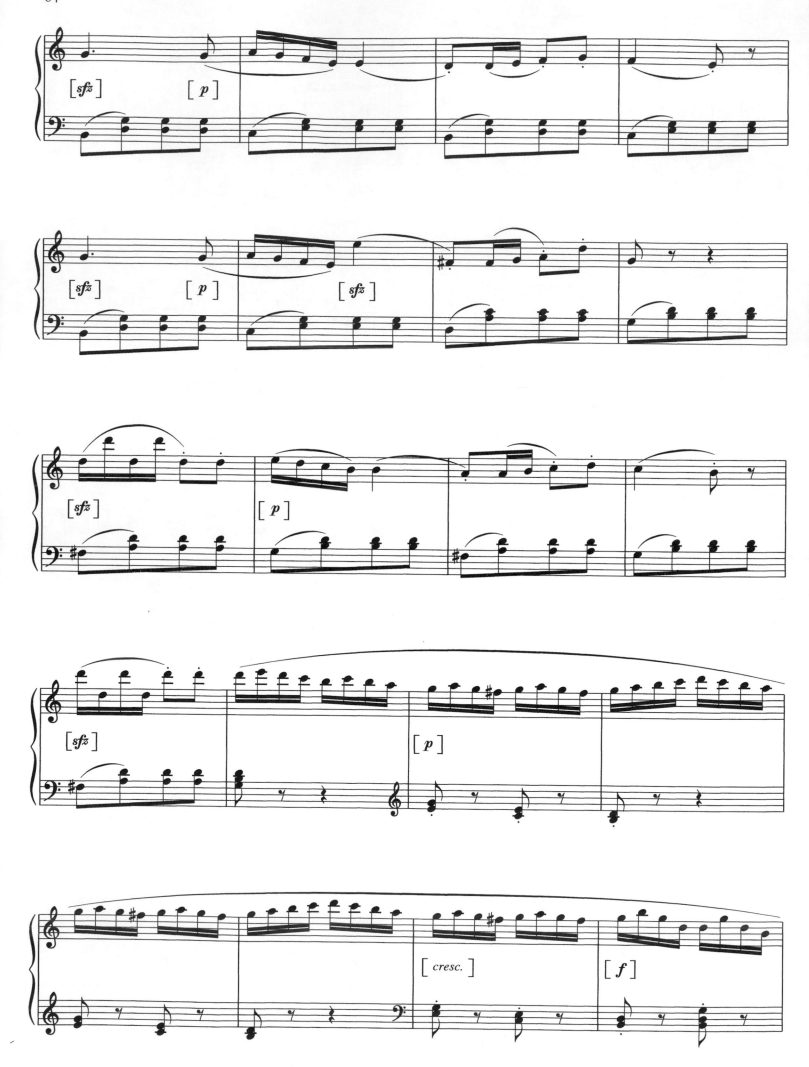

Arietta in C Major
from AN INTRODUCTION TO THE ART OF
PLAYING ON THE PIANOFORTE

Muzio Clementi
1752-1832
Op. 42

Allegretto

Spanish Dance

("Guaracha")
from AN INTRODUCTION TO THE ART OF
PLAYING ON THE PIANOFORTE

Muzio Clementi
1752-1832
Op. 42

Vivace

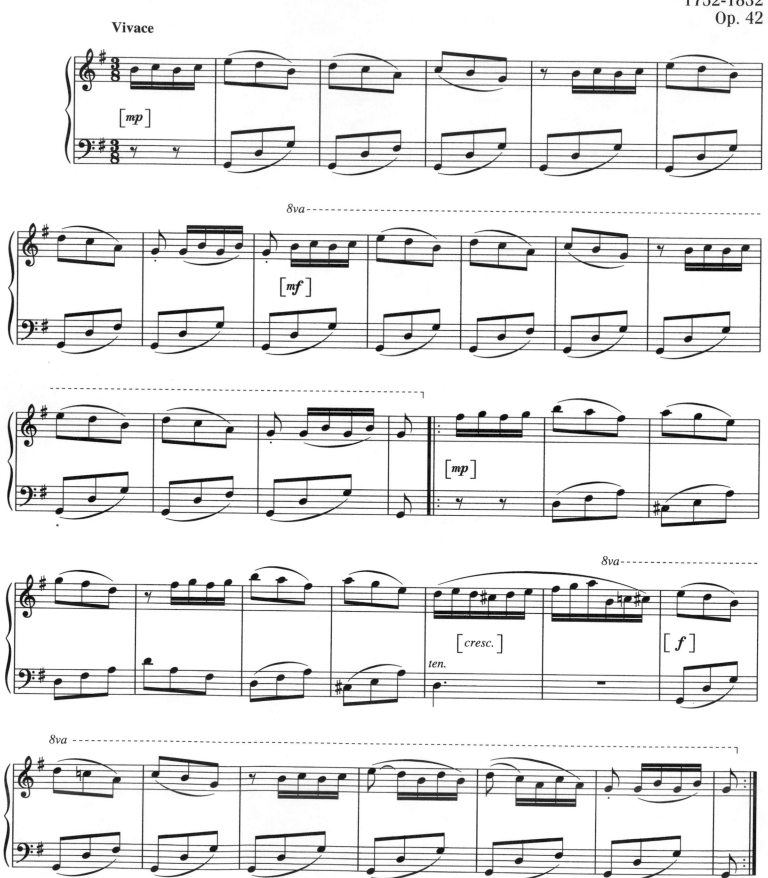

Sonatina

W. Duncombe
18th century

Allegretto

Spinning Song

(Spinnliedchen)

Albert Ellmenreich
1816-1905
Op. 14, No. 4

Allegretto

Album Leaf
from LYRIC PIECES, BOOK 1

Edvard Grieg
1843-1907
Op. 12, No. 7

Elves' Dance
from LYRIC PIECES, BOOK 1

Edvard Grieg
1843-1907
Op. 12, No.4

Molto Allegro e sempre staccato

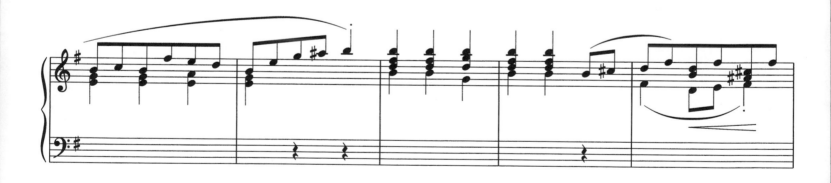

Waltz
from LYRIC PIECES, BOOK 1

Edvard Grieg
1843-1907
Op. 12, No. 2

Allegro moderato

Cradle Song
from LYRIC PIECES, BOOK 9

Edvard Grieg
1843-1907
Op. 68, No. 5

Allegretto tranquillamente

cresc. molto
fz
p
Ped.
ppp
poco rit.
a tempo
p
cresc.
*
Ped.
*
poco rit.
a tempo
molto
fz
molto
p la melodia ben ten.
8va
dim. e rit.
pp
ppp
Ped.
*
Ped. al Fine

Grandmother's Minuet

from LYRIC PIECES, BOOK 9

Edvard Grieg
1843-1907
Op. 68, No. 2

Allegretto grazioso e leggierissimo

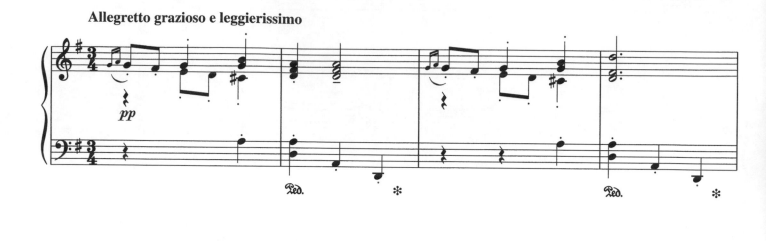

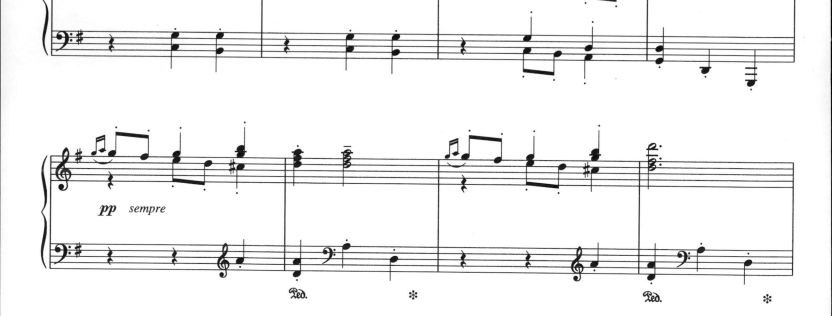

Tempo I

Sailor's Song
from LYRIC PIECES, BOOK 9

Edvard Grieg
1843-1907
Op. 68, No. 1

Allegro vivace e marcato

110

Dance in G Major

Joseph Haydn
1732-1809

Moderato

Allegro in F Major

Joseph Haydn
1732-1809

Sonata in C Major

Joseph Haydn
1732-1809
Hob. XVI:35

Allegro con brio

117

Adagio (Tempo I)

121

Finale
Allegro

126

Avalanche

Stephen Heller
1813-1888
Op. 45, No. 2

Allegro vivace

poco meno mosso

a tempo

Prelude in C Minor

Stephen Heller
1813-1888
Op. 119, No. 25

Etude in C Major

Stephen Heller
1813-1888
Op. 47, No. 19

Con moto (♩ = 192)
semplice e con grazia

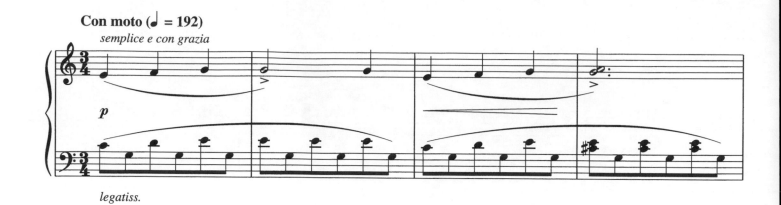

legatiss.

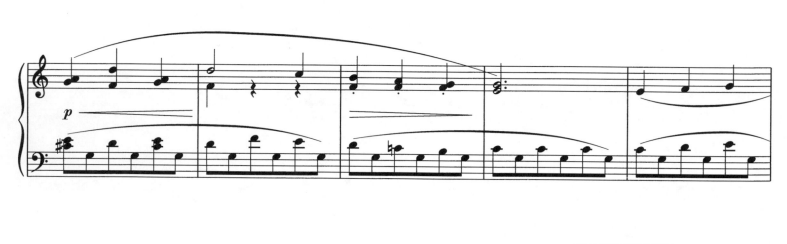

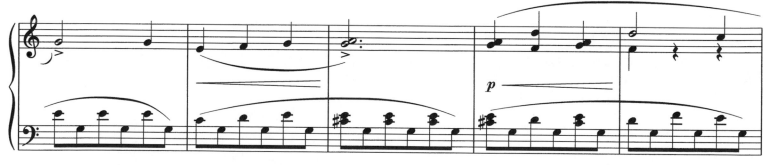

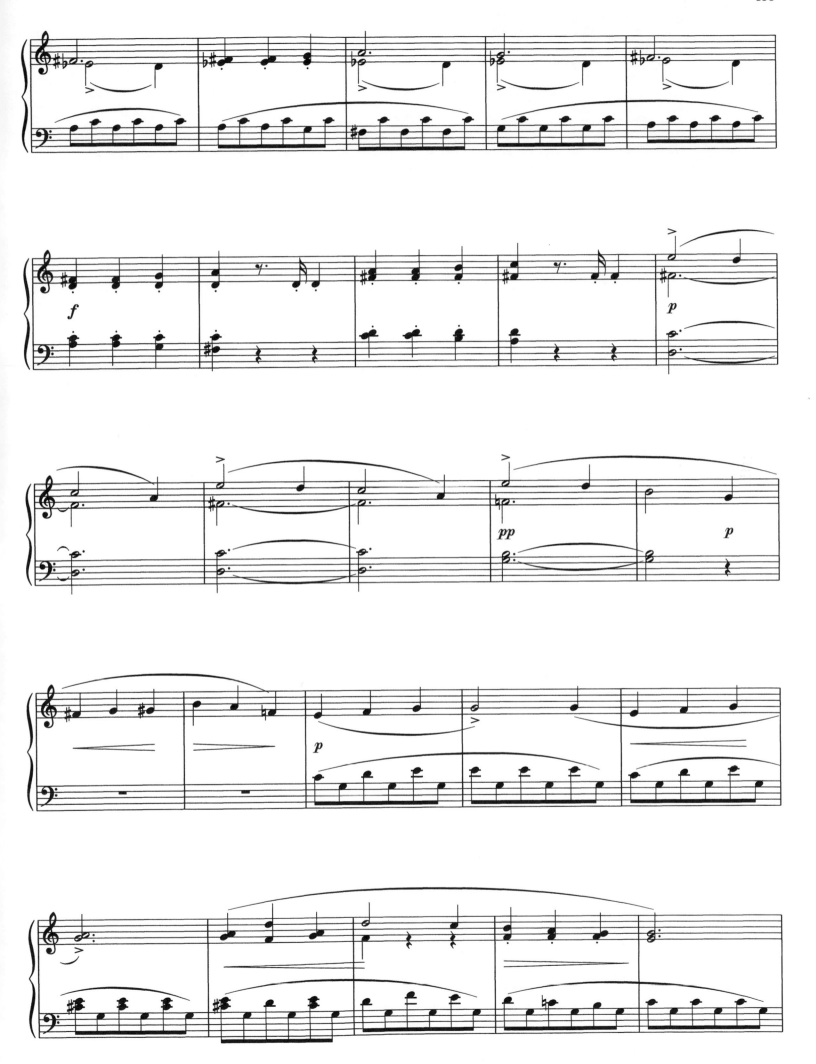

The Tolling Bell

Stephen Heller
1813-1888
Op. 125, No. 8

Esquisse

(Sketch)
from DOUZE ESQUISSES

Charles Koechlin
1867-1950
Op. 41

Allegretto e dolce

To a Wild Rose
from WOODLAND SKETCHES

Edward MacDowell
1860-1908
Op. 51

Confidence
from SONGS WITHOUT WORDS

Felix Mendelssohn
1809-1847
Op. 19, No. 4

Venetian Boat Song No. 1
from SONGS WITHOUT WORDS

Felix Mendelssohn
1809-1847
Op. 19, No. 6

Faith
from SONGS WITHOUT WORDS

Felix Mendelssohn
1809-1847
Op. 102, No. 6

Andante

Tarantella
from SONGS WITHOUT WORDS

Felix Mendelssohn
1809-1847
Op. 102, No. 3

Presto

Six Children's Pieces
(KINDERSTÜCKE)

Felix Mendelssohn
1809-1847
Op. 72

Allegro non troppo

1.

156

Andante con moto

4.

158

Allegro assai

5.

Allegro in B-flat Major

Wolfgang Amadeus Mozart
1756-1791
K. 3

[Allegro]

Minuet in C Major

Wolfgang Amadeus Mozart
1756-1791
K. 6

[Andante moderato]

(Fine)

Minuet in F Major

Wolfgang Amadeus Mozart
1756-1791
K. 2

Minuet in G Major

Wolfgang Amadeus Mozart
1756-1791
K. 1

Minuetto da Capo al Fine

Sonata in C Major

Domenico Scarlatti
1685-1757
L. 217 (K. 73b, P. 80)

Sonata in A Major

Domenico Scarlatti
1685-1757
L. 483 (K. 322, P. 360)

[Allegro]

[mf]

Sonata in D Minor

Domenico Scarlatti
1685-1757
L. 423 (K. 32, P. 14)

[Moderato]

(Fine)

Sonata in G Major

Domenico Scarlatti
1685-1757
L. 79 (K. 391, P. 364)

Ecossaise in D Major
(German Dance)

Franz Schubert
1797-1828
Op. 33, No. 2

[Moderato]

Moment Musicale

Franz Schubert
1797-1828
Op. 94, No. 3

Allegro moderato (♩ = 96)

il basso sempre staccato

Waltz in A-flat Major

Franz Schubert
1797-1828
Op. 9, No. 12

Waltz in G Major

Franz Schubert
1797-1828
Op. 67, No. 15

First Loss

from ALBUM FÜR DIE JUGEND

(Album for the Young)

Robert Schumann
1810-1856
Op. 68, No. 16

The Happy Farmer Returning from Work

(Frölicher Landmann, von der Arbeit zurückkehrend)

from ALBUM FÜR DIE JUGEND

(Album for the Young)

Robert Schumann
1810-1856
Op. 68, No. 10

Hunting Song
(Jägerliedchen)
from ALBUM FÜR DIE JUGEND
(Album for the Young)

Robert Schumann
1810-1856
Op. 68, No. 7

Vivace ♩. = 100

Melody

from ALBUM FÜR DIE JUGEND
(Album for the Young)

Robert Schumann
1810-1856
Op. 68, No. 1

Little Study

(Kleine Studie)

from ALBUM FÜR DIE JUGEND

(Album for the Young)

Robert Schumann
1810-1856
Op. 68, No. 14

The Reaper's Song

(Schnitterliedchen)
from ALBUM FÜR DIE JUGEND
(Album for the Young)

Robert Schumann
1810-1856
Op. 68, No. 18

Soldier's March

(Soldatenmarsch)
from ALBUM FÜR DIE JUGEND
(Album for the Young)

Robert Schumann
1810-1856
Op. 68, No. 2

Allegro deciso ♩ = 132

The Wild Horseman

(Wilder Reiter)
from ALBUM FÜR DIE JUGEND
(Album for the Young)

Robert Schumann
1810-1856
Op. 68, No. 8

Allegro con brio ♩. = 116

Cradle Song
(Wiegenliedchen)
from ALBUMBLÄTTER
(Album Leaves)

Robert Schumann
1810-1856
Op. 124, No. 6

197

A Child Falling Asleep
(Kind im Einschlummern)
from KINDERSZENEN
(Scenes from Childhood)

Robert Schumann
1810-1856
Op. 15, No. 12

Curious Story
(Curiose Geschichte)
from KINDERSZENEN
(Scenes from Childhood)

Robert Schumann
1810-1856
Op. 15, No. 2

Frightening

(Fürchtenmachen)
from KINDERSZENEN
(Scenes from Childhood)

Robert Schumann
1810-1856
Op. 15, No. 11

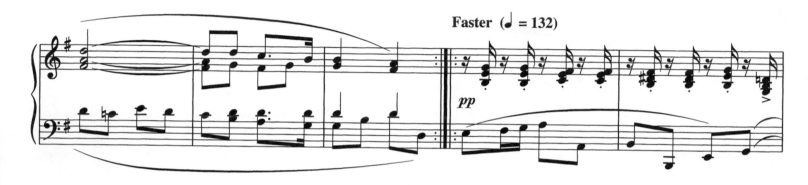

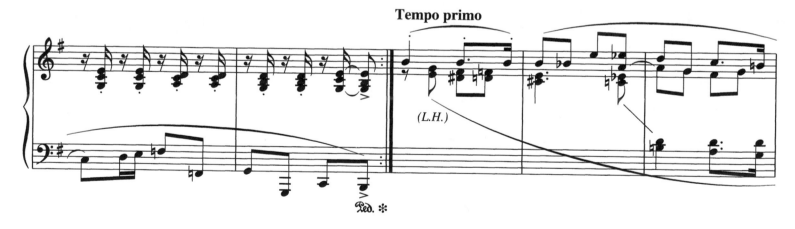

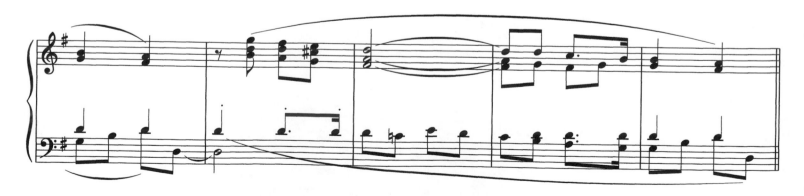

204

An Important Event

(Wichtige Begebenheit)

from KINDERSZENEN

(Scenes from Childhood)

Robert Schumann
1810-1856
Op. 15, No. 6

Copyright © 1998 by HAL LEONARD CORPORATION
International Copyright Secured   All Rights Reserved

Perfectly Contented

(Glückes genug)
from KINDERSZENEN
(Scenes from Childhood)

Robert Schumann
1810-1856
Op. 15, No. 5

Pleading Child
(Bittendes Kind)
from KINDERSZENEN
(Scenes from Childhood)

Robert Schumann
1810-1856
Op. 15, No. 4

The Poet Speaks

(Der Dichter spricht)

from KINDERSZENEN

(Scenes from Childhood)

Robert Schumann
1810-1856
Op. 15, No. 13

Träumerei

(Reverie)
from KINDERSZENEN
(Scenes from Childhood)

Robert Schumann
1810-1856
Op. 15, No. 7

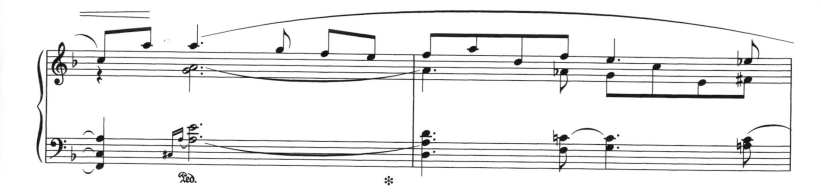

211

Of Strange Lands and People

(Von fremden Ländern und Menschen)

from KINDERSZENEN

(Scenes from Childhood)

Robert Schumann
1810-1856
Op. 15, No. 1

The Hobby Horse

(Le petit cavalier)

from ALBUM POUR ENFANTS

(Album for Children)

Pyotr Il'yich Tchaikovsky
1840-1893
Op. 39, No. 3

214

p sempre e staccatissimo

In Church

(A l'église)

from ALBUM POUR ENFANTS

(Album for Children)

Pyotr Il'yich Tchaikovsky
1840-1893
Op. 39, No. 24

Andantino (♩ = 58)

Italian Song
(Chanson italienne)
from ALBUM POUR ENFANTS
(Album for Children)

Pyotr Il'yich Tchaikovsky
1840-1893
Op. 39, No. 15

219

Old French Song

(Mélodie antique française)
from ALBUM POUR ENFANTS
(Album for Children)

Pyotr Il'yich Tchaikovsky
1840-1893
Op. 39, No. 16

The Organ Grinder

(L'orgue de barberie)

from ALBUM POUR ENFANTS

(Album for Children)

Pyotr Il'yich Tchaikovsky
1840-1893
Op. 39, No. 23

222

Polka
from ALBUM POUR ENFANTS
(Album for Children)

Pyotr Il'yich Tchaikovsky
1840-1893
Op. 39, No. 14

Moderato (♩ = 84)

Russian Song
(Chanson russe)
from ALBUM POUR ENFANTS
(Album for Children)

Pyotr Il'yich Tchaikovsky
1840-1893
Op. 39, No. 11

Allegro vivace (♩ = 152)

The Sick Doll

(La poupée malade)

from ALBUM POUR ENFANTS

(Album for Children)

Pyotr Il'yich Tchaikovsky
1840-1893
Op. 39, No. 6

The Song of the Lark

(Chant de l'alouette)

from ALBUM POUR ENFANTS

(Album for Children)

Pyotr Il'yich Tchaikovsky
1840-1893
Op. 39, No. 22

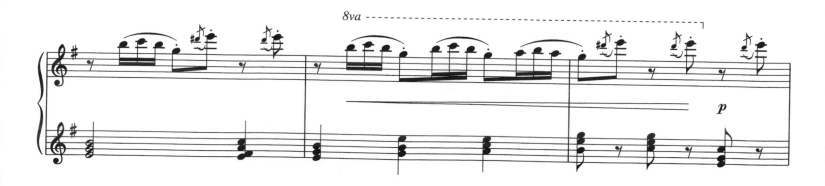

Sweet Dream
(Douce rêverie)
from ALBUM POUR ENFANTS
(Album for Children)

Pyotr Il'yich Tchaikovsky
1840-1893
Op. 39, No. 21

Dance

Georg Philipp Telemann
1681-1767

Allegretto

Little Rondo

Daniel Gottlob Türk
1750-1813